The Sales Minute

101 Tips for Retail Salespeople

Peter Smith

BookLocker
Saint Petersburg, Florida

Published by Booklocker.com, Inc.
e-mail: Dublinsmith@yahoo.com
Peter Smith on LinkedIn
www.TheRetailSmiths.com

Paperback ISBN: 978-1-64719-575-5
Hardcover ISBN: 978-1-64719-576-2
Ebook ISBN: 978-1-64719-577-9

Printed on acid-free paper.
Cover design by Todd Engel
Interior design by Ali Hibberts

Library of Congress Cataloging in Publication Data
Smith, Peter
The Sales Minute: 101 Tips for Retail Salespeople by Peter Smith
Library of Congress Control Number: 2021907670

Also by Peter Smith

Hiring Squirrels

12 Essential Interview Questions to Uncover Great Retail Sales Talent

Sell Something

Principles and Perspectives for Engaged Retail Salespeople

The Sales Minute

Sherry Smith inspires me every single day.

Her fingerprints are all over this book.

Table of Contents

The Sales Minute: 101 Tips for Retail Salespeople

Author's Note

According to the US Department of Labor Statistics, there are about 4.6 million salespeople in retail stores as of 2020. It is impossible to know how many of those salespeople are actively engaged in influencing customer behavior—as opposed to purely clerking.

However, any visit to better-quality retail environments such as jewelers, clothing stores, shoe stores, department store makeup counters, furniture stores etc., reveals that there are a great many salespeople who have the opportunity to inspire consumer behavior and who believe themselves to be committed sales professionals.

This book is for them.

My goal was to write a book that would serve as a companion piece for salespeople who are interested in their own professional development. A book that doesn't necessarily need to be read from cover to cover but can be opened randomly to provide a tip or pointer to be put into practice that day.

The short-format approach with this book is new for me and, I confess, quite challenging. There is so much material and research on the psychology of sales, and I am more accustomed to writing columns and articles that present those findings in a narrative form, with appropriate attribution and suggested reading. That was certainly true of my previous books, *Hiring Squirrels* and *Sell Something*, where I used storytelling to engage the reader.

This book is different, and I hope you will enjoy its shorter format. I had intended to call it *Tweet-Sized Tips* but ultimately concluded that many of the tips needed to be expanded beyond the current 280-character format on Twitter.

The list of topics is comprehensive but not exhaustive. I have no doubt that other writers and training professionals could produce an additional 101 tips from just those topics I've missed. That said, *202 Sales Tips* just doesn't have the same ring to it.

Excepting the first couple of points, the book is expressly not sequential. It can be read in one sitting or consumed in more digestible bites, one tip at a time.

Whichever route you choose, I hope you enjoy the ride.

Peter Smith

Love Your Work

Everyone has good days and bad, colleagues we like more than others, managers who inspire and managers who don't.

Studies show that as many as 50 percent of people in the US are not engaged in their work, and another 20 percent are actively disengaged.

If you are energized by human connection, by the challenges of helping people, and by the desire to make sales and keep score, you will more readily find purpose and fulfillment in your work as a salesperson.

Notwithstanding the natural ebbs and flows of any position, loving your job is the single most important ingredient for happiness, success, and mental well-being.

Loving your job does not mean you never have bad days or disappointments, but it does mean that your work aligns with your innate wiring and personality—and that is a critical ingredient for sales success.

Authenticity

Authenticity has become a buzzword, but what does it really mean? Aren't we all authentic versions of ourselves? In reality, many of us invest too much time trying to be somebody we're not. We suppress our authentic selves to please bosses, colleagues, and friends, and often put ourselves in situations, socially and professionally, that don't align with our genuine selves.

We can all demonstrate chameleon-like characteristics for a short time. However, if the face you present is not really you, it is neither believable nor sustainable because your body-language will communicate your discomfort and unease.

Being authentic does not mean the absence of filters to ensure social norms and conventions. It does, however, mean the environment we commit ourselves to aligns with our natural wiring so that we can bring our best and honest selves to work each and every day.

Don't Information Dump

Have you ever wondered why the best salespeople are not always the most well-versed about your products' features and benefits? Have you ever found yourself scratching your head watching a new salesperson make a big sale without mastering the nuances of your products?

What great salespeople know is that sales is about triggering emotions, not taxing customers with irrelevant details and unnecessary facts.

Our brain weighs two or three pounds, yet requires 20 percent of our body's energy to function. Its primary mission is to not overly tax itself - and there is no better example of that than watching a customer disengage in the middle of a product diatribe.

It is important to know your products well enough to speak to them, but the goal is to connect on an emotional level, not to impress customers with your brilliant cognitive recall.

Don't Overuse "I"

Overusing the word "I" when talking to customers is a bad idea. It can come across as self-serving, perhaps even a little arrogant. It also suggests that you alone bought the merchandise, built the store, and are paying all the bills.

We don't work in a vacuum, and we should never act like we do. Use the word *we* whenever possible to let the customer know they are dealing with more than a single individual.

It is reassuring for customers to know that they have the store's team behind them for the long haul, especially given the high turnover in many retail stores.

Make Eye Contact

We process visuals about ten times faster than words, so while what we say matters, what we see will have hit home long before any words are spoken or understood.

Making eye contact with customers is not only good manners but good science. Staring directly into someone's eyes generates electrical activity in their brain, which increases their heart rate, making it easier to build a genuine emotional connection.

When you are speaking, hold your eye contact for at least four seconds or until your sentence or idea has been communicated. When your customer is speaking, maintain eye contact until they have finished their thought, idea, or question.

A Great Sales Experience Means
Someone Bought Something

If I had a dollar for every time a salesperson said, "They'll be back," I'd be a rich man.

A successful interaction is one that results in a satisfied customer, a happy salesperson, and something having been purchased.

That's how the bills get paid, and there should be no doubting that selling something is the minimum objective with every customer contact.

Sales "math" will, of course, dictate that no salesperson, no matter how talented, will turn every single prospect into a sale, but that should still be the objective.

Anything less is a missed opportunity.

Using Humor

Humor has played a key role in evolution, relieving stress, lowering blood pressure, and providing a coping mechanism in difficult moments. It is also a terrific way to make a human connection and break the ice when meeting customers.

Sales is not the place to practice your stand-up routine but wearing a smile on your face and demonstrating humility and warmth, with a little self-effacing humor, can endear you to your customers and help mitigate minor stresses and awkward silences.

Remember, people are more likely to buy from someone they like and bringing a smile to your customer's face will always be a positive development.

Open-Ended Questions

Getting the customer to do the talking is always a sound idea, and open-ended questions are the best way to make that happen.

Questions such as "Tell me about..." or "What is it that you..." or "What's most important to you about..." cannot be answered with yes or no.

Make yourself a list of questions that can help get the customer talking about things that matter to them, and avoid any rote ("Are you looking for something in particular today?") or yes-or-no questions.

Work your list of questions, and refine them as needed for maximum effectiveness. Not all questions will fit all salespeople, so it is a good idea to try yours for fit and tweak as you go.

Don't Lie

It would seem to be patently obvious to suggest that we should not tell lies, even little white ones, in a sales environment, but it needs to be said and it should be heeded.

When you are not being truthful, your body language, gestures, eye contact, and general physicality will be incongruous with your words, and your customer will sense the disconnect.

Even if they do not believe you are outright lying, they will feel uneasy at the discordant nature of your overall demeanor.

Be straight-up with your customers, and they'll thank you for it.

Smile

When you smile in an authentic way, you trigger mirror neurons in the person you are engaged with. Customers don't particularly care why you are smiling; they're simply happy that you are doing so, and they are more likely to reciprocate and adopt a more positive attitude toward you. Their positive attitude will then charge your mirror neurons and make you feel happier and more connected.

If you need evidence of how authentic smiling can be communicated with your eyes, the ubiquitous mask-wearing of COVID-19 provided ample proof of that. Despite covering our mouths, we were able to quickly identify warm smiles just by looking into each other's eyes.

We don't have a finite number of smiles in our arsenal, so give them out freely.

We'll all be better for it.

Be Curious

A curious salesperson has two important attributes: the humility to accept that he or she does not have all the answers, and the desire to learn develop personally and professionally.

There are many ways to satisfy your curiosity. That might be done formally, by taking classes, pursuing credentials in your field, reading books and articles, watching TED talks, or listening to podcasts.

It can also include watching, emulating, and learning from top performers in your own organization— perhaps the greatest learning of all.

The Paradox of Choice

As counterintuitive as it seems, choice is not always a good thing, at least beyond a certain point.

Presenting too many options increases the cognitive burden for the customer. So much so, in fact, that he or she will remove themselves from any conversation that requires them to think too much or work too hard.

If you have done your job in engaging the customer and understand her motivations and needs, limiting the number of options to three is the best thing you can do for her.

Being presented with three options allows her to feel ownership in the decision-making process—a central tenet in human psychology—without overwhelming her.

Dress the Part

Never underestimate the transformative power of rituals, and one of the most powerful rituals is choosing how we dress each morning.

In the simple act of selecting our attire for work, we begin the transformation into professional mode as we prepare for the day ahead. The change is both psychological and physiological. If we look the part, we feel the part.

Fewer stores today seem to have dress codes, but if you need a rule of thumb, here it is: if you are dressing more casually than your average customer, you're probably underdressing.

If it is possible to do so, fly your club colors. Wearing your store's products is the best way to advocate for them and sends a clear single to your prospects that you believe in what you are selling.

Mimic Verbals and Nonverbals

Synchronizing your tone of voice, facial expressions, and body language with your customer's is an effective yet largely unconscious way to create rapport.

Our brains are hardwired to sync with others (getting thrown out of the cave back in the day was a dangerous proposition), and we are more likely to trust people who mirror our gestures, vocal intonations, and physicality.

Quickly observe your customer's demeanor (hurried, relaxed, quiet, louder, formal, informal, etc.) and align your behavior and demeanor accordingly. It can and should be done in a subtle way, but the payoff in connectivity can be profound.

Emotion Sells

Even the most cursory reading on the psychology of buying will reveal that customers buy emotionally, not logically.

If you are trying to sell to customers based on logic, rationale, and your cognitive prowess, you won't engage the limbic connection in your customer's brain, the area that really makes the decision. You will also increase the likelihood of your customer shutting you down and taking their business elsewhere.

In a high-profile study of customer buying behaviors, the data showed customers who bought emotionally delivered a 23 percent premium on the sale, whereas customers who bought logically delivered a 13 percent discount.

As Oscar Wilde once opined, "Man is many things, but he is not rational."

Body Language Videos

Research shows that 55 percent of communication is physiological, so understanding the basics of body language can be a game changer.

People sometimes make the mistake of wishing to be experts at reading customers' body language when they would be better off understanding what their own nonverbals are communicating to the customer.

Your body language sets the tone for customer interactions long before you open your mouth to say anything.

Find some TED talks on body language and put some of the teachings into practice. Amy Cuddy has a particularly good TED talk that you might find helpful.

Contrast Principle

When a customer gives you a price range, use the price as the lowest option of three.

For instance, if she says $500, the three options you present should be $500, $750, and $1000.

The lower amount validates the customer's stated price, and the highest amount sets an anchor by which the other options are viewed.

The customer will be satisfied that their stated price was offered as an option. They will use the highest price (the anchor) to judge the relative accessibility of the middle price, and that, more often than not, will be the option selected.

In short, the two extremes—high and low—make the middle option more appealing and more likely to be chosen.

Author's Note: This segment works best when combined with The Paradox of Choice on page 24.

How You Say Price Matters

How you *say* a price can change a customer's perception of that price.

Crazy, I know, but studies show that to be the case. The more syllables used in verbally quoting the price, the higher the price is perceived to be.

For instance, "One thousand, five hundred, and fifty dollars" will be perceived as a higher price than "Fifteen fifty."

Likewise, a price with a comma, such as $1,550.00 will be perceived as higher than $1550.

When quoting price, condition yourself to use fewer syllables.

A Bias to Action

Sales is not a passive occupation.

Successful salespeople have a bias to action. They are perpetually in motion, hunting for opportunities and keeping their pipeline filled with prospects and repeat customers.

They prioritize direct and indirect selling activities, and they eschew non-selling responsibilities to the point that it can be exasperating to their less sales-oriented colleagues and their managers.

In short, superlative salespeople wake up in the morning ready for action.

Show Your Favorite Products

Authenticity communicates, so if you are genuinely enthusiastic about certain products, it holds that the customer will sense your belief and respond accordingly.

Pre-select a range of products in different categories, and at different price points, and show them with reverence and respect.

Note that your selected products must align with what you learn about the customer in your open-ended questions and your back-and-forth dialogue, but familiarizing yourself with a range of products will make your story more fluid and believable.

Movement

Don't allow yourself to be stationary for too long as it doesn't translate well for customers entering your store.

From the earliest evolutionary days, when our ancestors traversed the Serengeti, our brains have been wired to respond to movement. It was, quite simply, how we found dinner, and it was also how we avoided becoming dinner.

Fast forward seven million years or so, and our primal brains are still drawn to three-dimensional movement.

Standing behind a counter, inside the front door, or at the back of the store behind a service desk is not likely to draw the attention or interest of a customer.

Movement matters, and it should always be in the customer's field of view, directly or peripherally, not from behind.

Negative People

There is no value whatsoever in choosing to associate with chronically negative people.

We all have an occasional bad day or a tough moment when we need to vent, but some people seem to have been born to complain, and they must be avoided at all costs.

Negativity begets negativity, and the endless cycle of complaining, underperformance, and anticipated and realized disappointment becomes self-fulfilling, not just for the complainer, but for people within their orbit who allow themselves to be pulled into the emotional abyss.

Choose carefully who you spend time with and avoid or limit your exposure to negative people.

Your sanity will thank you for it.

Tell Stories

Storytelling is the glue that emotionally connects salespeople and customers, and every salesperson should have a repertoire of stories that can be accessed as needed to engage clients.

When you tell stories, the mirror neurons in your customer's brain ignite, and you more quickly become synchronous. The stories need to be short, relevant, and, most importantly, authentic.

Today's conversations are tomorrow's stories, so collect them, catalog them—this is as easy as opening a note on your phone and inserting a trigger to remind you of a good story that can be used in a given situation—and use them when they make sense.

The stories should speak to how you've worked with customers to help them solve their challenges.

Remember, customers don't want a litany of facts and features, and please spare them the industry jargon.

Experience Means Nothing If You Don't Do the Right Stuff

There is a vast difference between someone with ten years of work experience and someone who has one year's worth of experience repeated ten times.

It speaks to the myth of the ten thousand hours—the idea that merely doing something for ten thousand hours equates to expertise.

Swedish psychologist, Anders Ericsson, internationally recognized for his life's work on expertise in human performance, was quite specific in noting that expert performance requires more than just the distinction of having worked ten thousand hours in a given job.

Expert performance requires purposeful and deliberate practice. It demands specific and repeated actions designed to push you out of your comfort zone. It calls for an embrace of discomfort itself, to discover new ways of doing things and constant learning to drive through barriers and obstacles on your path to mastery, whether you have ten years of experience or one.

Distracted Listening

As often as we are reminded of the importance of maintaining eye contact and giving our undivided attention, we hear less about the potentially destructive consequences of distracted listening.

Breaking eye contact with a customer sends a signal that you have lost interest and would rather be doing something else, and the impact of that distraction is more damaging to a shared experience than a heated argument.

Be completely present when you are listening to a customer and break eye contact, with an apology, only when absolutely unavoidable.

Show Product with Reverence

Always show your products with great reverence and respect.

What you say will matter little if you handle the product in an overtly carefree manner, and treating your products as undifferentiated commodities invites the customer to do likewise.

You are conducting visual theater, and the highest compliment you can pay your customer is to present your products with care and consideration.

You are, in effect, showing the customer how to interact with the product.

Hand Gestures

Effective communicators use their hands more when they are speaking. It makes them appear warmer and more relatable.

People who hide their hands, hold them in a static position, or keep them in their pockets are perceived as less engaging and perhaps even threatening. This goes back to our evolutionary genesis when we needed to see the hands of approaching strangers to determine if they were carrying a weapon.

Practice using your hands to communicate. Watch TED talks and notice how often the best communicators use their hands.

In a post-pandemic world, when shaking hands may become less ubiquitous, showing and using your hands to communicate will be more important than ever.

Admit You Don't Know

There might be worse things than watching a salesperson stumble and bumble their way through a customer question they clearly are not prepared for, but I can't think of one at this moment.

Nobody is expected to know everything, and the world of sales is no different. Customers rightfully expect a level of proficiency, but they'll usually be understanding if a salesperson asks them to wait a moment while they find the answer to their question.

They may even be prepared for you to call, text, or email them a follow-up if you can't find the answer while they are in the store.

Taking ownership and demonstrating a little humility is a better strategy than providing half-truths and pretending you know something you don't.

Use Touch

I'm writing this segment in the middle of a global pandemic when we are all practicing social distancing. That said, when it is safe to do so, the power of touch cannot be emphasized strongly enough.

The healing properties of touch, emotionally and as a stress-reliever, are aided by nerve fibers in our skin designed expressly to respond to human touch.

We see the effects from the time we are babies, and the comforting aspects of human touch are no less soothing as we age.

From shaking hands to touching someone's arm, elbow, or shoulder, there are numerous opportunities in sales environments to touch your customers appropriately to help forge a physiological connection.

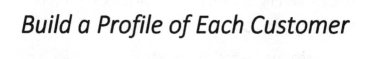

Build a Profile of Each Customer

Over the course of meetings with your customers, you should learn a great deal about them: likes, dislikes, family or work tidbits, hobbies, etc. Make a note of what you learn and build a profile for each customer.

Having emails and phone numbers is a great way to facilitate future engagement, and the content you submit will be all the more relevant if you have created a more robust profile.

Getting the details can be as easy as asking for them, especially if you have promised to follow up with requested information, or to communicate new product arrivals, sales, or customer-appreciation events.

Customers are often willing to provide contact information if there is something in it for them.

Expect to Close Every Sale

Top salespeople judge themselves against their own high standards. They know they won't close every sale, but it doesn't stop them from approaching every customer with the expectation of doing just that.

If you believe you won't close every sale, that mindset becomes a self-fulfilling prophecy that can negatively impact your performance and wreak havoc on your closing percentages.

Stellar sales performance is a product of a positive mindset. If you expect to close every sale—as statistically unlikely as it may be—that expectation will fuel and elevate your sales performance.

Show Your Passion

Positive emotions travel, so if you genuinely feel excited about what you do, your products, and your company, that passion will influence your customer's perception of you and your business.

The authenticity of your passion will communicate in your body language, in your eyes and smile, and in your tone of voice, and will surmount any verbal messaging.

As long as your passion is genuine, it will ignite your customers' mirror neurons so that you and your customer become synchronic.

Regret as Motivator

When customers contemplate a purchase, one of the most important, albeit unconscious, considerations are anticipated regrets about not making the right choice, or not making any decision at all.

When people are asked about their regrets, they indicate by a margin of two to one regret of inaction more than regret of actions taken that might not have turned out as well as they'd hoped.

While people are more likely to move on from bad choices, they hold onto regrets about the things they did not do for years or even decades.

A simple sentence such as "This is an important purchase, and you won't regret this choice" can unconsciously remind the buyer that his real motivation in buying is not just to avoid making a bad choice but, in fact, to avoid inaction itself.

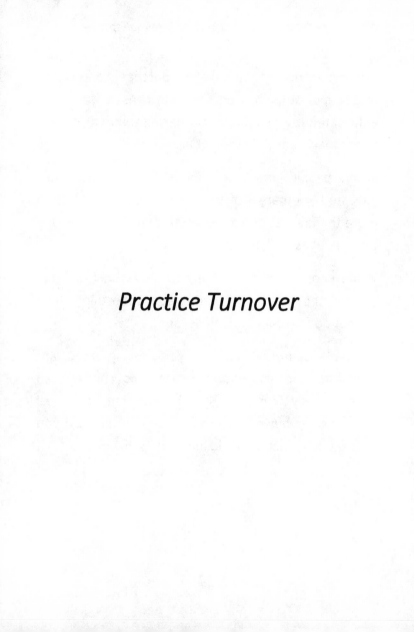

Practice Turnover

Studies show that when we meet someone, we make decisions about them in one-tenth of one second. Given that, the notion that any one salesperson will connect with every single customer they meet is egotism personified.

Unfortunately, some salespeople see turnover as a personal failure and having to give the customer to a colleague as salt in their wounds. That is not the case.

There are many reasons why a customer might feel uncomfortable with a salesperson, and most of them are not remotely conscious, so plan to turn over customers when the dynamic seems off, whether you've just greeted them or have worked with them for a few minutes.

Practice "pulling in the expert" as you introduce the customer to your colleague when you feel like someone else might better connect.

Ask for the Sale

If you have done your job creating a rapport with your customer (listening, asking open-ended questions, etc.), you must ask for the sale.

More business is lost because salespeople assume customers will let them know when they are ready to make a purchase, and that simply isn't the case.

In fact, some studies show that as many as 70 percent of customers make a purchase when they are asked to do so, and yet many retail stores convert only 20 to 30 percent of their prospects into sales.

Customers don't always want to slow-walk the process, exhausting every option, visiting multiple retail stores, and checking all online options before making their decision. Sometimes they just want the salesperson to do his or her job and confidently and respectfully ask the sale.

Customer Outreach

One of the great fallacies of retail is that stores are reactive businesses; customers decide when they will visit, and salespeople react when they do. That, of course, is simply not true.

Every customer contact—and especially every time a sale is made—is an opportunity to gather contact information, and those customers should be touched on a regular basis thereafter.

Top salespeople understand the power of outreach. They know that to be successful they cannot operate reactively, waiting for customers to come into their stores. They invest in client outreach initiatives on a regular basis to drive qualified customers into their stores.

Gather customer information. Ask the customer for permission to follow up with new product information, trunk shows or events, sales or customer appreciation evenings, and ask the customer what his or her preferred contact method is.

Choose Optimism

Optimism is a brain-based coping strategy that enables us to keep going in the face of disappointments and failures.

It is hardwired into our brains, but it can be improved with practice.

Optimists play a disproportionate role in shaping the world we live in. They are the people who invent stuff, the entrepreneurs who build innovative companies, the people who sell the toughest ideas to the most entrenched naysayers, and they are the best salespeople.

Choosing optimism is good for our mental and physical well-being, and it provides the fuel to overcome even the toughest logic-based arguments.

In short, people (customers and colleagues) prefer optimists.

Thank-You Notes

It is a rare salesperson who sends a handwritten note anymore.

Doing so will make you stand out for all the right reasons. A simple "Thank you for your business" can go a long way toward building a longer-term relationship.

At a minimum, you should send a thank-you note to your customers, be it via text, email, or even via LinkedIn or Facebook. It's also wise to call after the fact, to ask how the product worked out.

A written note of appreciation sends a very warm and personal message that will stand out in an age of digital overload.

Failure to thank a customer for his or her business is bad business.

Be Passionate about Learning

Constant learning is the greatest gift you can give yourself as a salesperson.

Studies have shown that when we struggle to learn, when we demonstrate a willingness to put ourselves in challenging situations, it literally changes the composition of our brains, making the learning stickier and more beneficial long-term.

There are so many sources of learning today, and content can be consumed in digestible bites at a time and place that suits any schedule.

Invest in yourself and feed your brain's natural craving for learning and development.

Set Goals for Yourself

Having goals is like having a GPS for your own performance.

The most obvious examples are daily, weekly, and monthly sales goals. Top-line sales performance is the easiest metric to drive business, and it is usually the most transparent. After all, in sales, the scorecard will always matter.

But there are other measures to drive your performance. What is your average sale? How many units can you sell in a day? Can you improve your personal conversion rate? Can you sell x amount of add-on sales? How many customers do you prospect on a daily basis?

And, if this information is shared with you, what are your bottom-line profitability goals?

Most sales organizations set sales goals to establish performance guardrails. If your store is one of the rare businesses that declines to implement and share sales goals, set your own and measure yourself daily.

Use Your Colleagues

Everyone brings something different to the table, and utilizing your colleagues is a great way to show them respect. Of course, it cannot be a one-way street, so make sure to offer your help to them when the opportunity presents itself.

A coworker may not have your acumen, sales drive, or resilience, but they may have great product knowledge, a better understanding of procedures or practices, or a particularly strong opening when greeting customers.

Asking your colleagues to help you demonstrates humility and curiosity. A simple question such as "What do you think?" or "What would you do in that situation?" is a powerful way to build rapport and reinforce a culture of cooperation and respect.

Promote Advocacy

If you have provided good service to your customers, you should ask them to provide referrals for your business.

This can be as simple as giving them a couple of extra business cards to pass along or asking them to leave a Google or Yelp review, a note on their social media pages, etc.

This is particularly true in my business (jewelry), where young people buying engagement rings will usually have a network that includes peers who might soon be in a similar situation and thinking about getting engaged.

Getting customers to advocate for your store is quite simply the highest form of promotion.

Don't be shy about asking for the advocacy. People are usually happy to help if they feel good about how they were treated in a business, but they might not always do so if you don't ask.

Inspire Buying Behavior

The North Star for a salesperson is to inspire buying behavior... that's how the bills get paid!

The most successful salespeople do so by engaging their customers' primal brain, the bottom half of the brain, the part that has the greatest influence in their decision-making process.

They inspire and influence their customers by getting them emotionally invested, by helping them visualize how and where the product will be used, and by inviting the customer to consider what the response of the recipient might be if the purchase is a gift.

Inspiring your customers with your passion, your belief, and your authenticity helps them feel an emotional connection to you, your product, and your store.

Sell Value, Not Price

Value and price are separate and often confused terms.

If I buy something for the cheapest price and it breaks or underperforms, did I get good value? Of course not.

If I pay more for something than I might have wished, and it performs beautifully for years, did I pay too much?

Establishing value requires the salesperson to understand the underlying motivations behind a customer's questions and to probe beneath surface-level requests for cheaper prices and/or discounts.

Customers will sometimes default to a request for lower prices as a negotiation tactic, or because they are really asking the salesperson to sell them on the value proposition.

Do the necessary work, and sell the customer something he or she won't regret buying.

That's value.

Shaking Hands

Handshaking is a good way to build trust when we meet someone for the first time.

When we shake hands, we release a chemical called oxytocin that makes the pleasantness of touch very comforting.

The handshake should be firm and be accompanied by good eye-contact and an authentic smile.

You will not impress anyone with a knuckle-breaking death grip, and limp handshakes are an absolute turnoff that should be avoided at all costs.

In a post-pandemic environment, some customers might prefer a little space and eschew handshaking altogether, while others will see it as perfectly acceptable.

Use your best judgment and allow the customer to take the lead before reaching for her hand.

Mini Product Groupings

Pre-selecting a range of mini product groupings utilizing the paradox of choice (page 24) and the contrast principle (page 35) can be an effective way to present product options to your customers.

A good way to position your mini-stories might be to assemble a few choices in different products by price range. A few examples might include:

A. $500 budget, show $500, $750, $1000 options.

B. $1000 budget, show $1000, $1,500, $2000 options.

C. $5000 budget, show $5000, $7500, $10,000 options.

Selecting product groupings in advance and presenting them by price point as needed provides great options for your customers that utilizes important psychological principles.

Own Your Mistakes

Making mistakes is a necessary condition for professional growth and development.

You simply cannot push yourself beyond your boundaries and limitations unless you are willing to try new ways of doing things, and that means you will mess up once in a while.

When it happens, it doesn't always feel good. In fact, it sometimes feels like it will derail us in profound ways.

Most mistakes, however, are rarely fatal, but they are always good teachers if we are willing to correct them and learn from them.

The easiest way to avoid making mistakes is to try nothing new, to settle for an attitude and approach that is so safe and predictable that it becomes impossible to grow.

Lean into your mistakes and accept that they will occasionally be uncomfortable but always enlightening.

Be Confident, Not Arrogant

Confidence expressed in both words and deeds—and supported with humility and empathy—is an extremely attractive quality to customers and colleagues alike.

No one appreciates a know-it-all braggart, and that is particularly off-putting when the "expert" lacks self-awareness.

Be confident in your ability and willingness to help others, and refrain from projecting arrogance.

A quiet confidence is much more reassuring to people than a lecture on everything you know.

Your Education in Twenty Minutes

There is a big difference between someone who works in retail and someone who is a sales professional in a retail environment—and most of it has to do with self-view.

Sales professionals see themselves as serious and committed to their work, and they look to better themselves at their craft—the craft of sales.

If you are serious about your career development, it should be worth twenty minutes of your time each day. That's a chapter in a book, a podcast, a training video, or a thoughtful article from LinkedIn. In short, it has never been easier to find relevant content if you are inspired to do so.

Learning activates the reward centers in our brains and helps to keep us mentally fresh and engaged.

Make learning a habit, and put what you learn into practice that day.

Sell What's Healthy for the Business

In a perfect world, all products in a store would be equally profitable. That, however, is rarely the case.

Out of necessity, many stores carry products that on their own would not provide enough profit to sustain the business.

The brands or products are deemed necessary to support the broader business objective but can, if they consume a too-large portion of the sales, place a drain on margins and profitability.

Blindly reaching for those products, especially if they are at lower price points or loss leaders, can put an unnecessary strain on the business.

Salespeople should know what categories, brands, or products are deemed essential to the profitability of the business and ensure that those products are front and center when they align with the customer's needs.

Pessimists Are Right—a Lot

Pessimism is a self-fulfilling prophecy.

If you believe bad things will happen, customers won't buy, deliveries will be late, products won't perform, you're going to orient your expectations accordingly and unwittingly condition yourself to expect the worst.

Pessimism is not nearly as much fun as optimism. It is not good for your physical or mental health, and it doesn't engender the best relationships with customers, colleagues, or your manager, but being a pessimist means you'll be right a lot.

Psychologists use the term "defensive pessimism" to describe how some people set low expectations for themselves. Subsequently, when their low expectations are met, they have an easier time dealing with the consequences because they had little expectation of success in the first place.

You will not be great in sales if you are a pessimist.

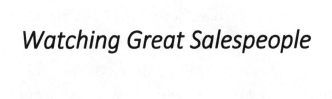

Watching Great Salespeople

Great salespeople have lots in common, drive, resilience, empathy, and optimism being chief amongst them. Each, however, has their own preferred methods, processes, and approaches with customers. Watching and learning from them is a master class of sorts.

Carefully observing their specific steps in approaching customers, overcoming objections, handling resistance, and closing sales can be enlightening.

It might mean observing the preparation they put into their day, how they prospect new customers and follow up with existing customers and noting the obsessive nature in how they advocate for their customers in their own organizations is all very telling.

Whether you partner with a winner formally, or informally watch them, is for each individual to decide.

But ignore them - and the valuable lessons they provide - at your peril.

Rejection Shouldn't Define You

No salesperson likes to hear a customer say no.

It's hard for it not to feel personal. In fact, it should feel personal.

This is what you do for a living, and feeling like you gave it your best effort without getting the desired result should never feel good.

That said, rejection should not define you. It should not consume you to the point that you become reluctant to ask the next customer for the sale.

Salespeople who lack resilience can experience great anxiety from not making a sale. So much so that they spend less time in front of customers and even less time asking for the sale when they do.

Great salespeople don't like rejection, but they know that it is a necessary evil in any sales job. It is not an indictment of them personally. It is simply a part of the sales process, and they learn from the disappointment and move on to the next customer with no loss of positivity or enthusiasm.

Send the Elevator Back Down

There are very few people who are accomplished in their field who did not get a helping hand from someone along the way.

Sometimes it takes years before we realize how beneficial a given relationship was, but there is always someone who helped, knowingly or unknowingly, formally, or informally.

Pay it forward and give the benefit of your experience to someone in your business. You don't have to be their manager to mentor a colleague, and the satisfaction from helping someone else do better can be extremely rewarding.

*To Avoid Criticism, Try
Nothing New*

On some level, we all suffer from what psychologists call the "status quo bias." It means that we have a default orientation to continue to do what is familiar and easy for us, rather than driving ourselves out of our comfort zones.

Professional growth means that we must push through our boundaries to try new things, even as we know that doing so will bring discomfort, disorientation, and, on occasion, even outright failures. The best learning comes from the grit and courage needed to try new things.

As a committed and serious sales professional, you should be prepared to try new things from time to time: a new way to engage customers, new language, different nonverbals, or new ideas you witnessed when you yourself were shopping.

Don't Spend from Your Pocket

The reason we explore our customers' motivations, needs, and desires is to understand what they want and, in the process, to understand what value proposition is most important to them.

Customers bring all sorts of psychological triggers into their shopping experiences, and we cannot make assumptions about what those triggers are without doing the work.

Believing that your customers see value the same way you do is a mistake that is devoid of context and presumptuous.

Do your job in uncovering their motivations and don't spend from your own pocket.

Leaning In

Leaning in when you are listening to, or speaking with, a customer demonstrates your engagement and curiosity.

It is a wonderfully physical indicator of interest, intent, and empathy, and it should be subtle enough that it sits just below the level of consciousness for your customer.

Be mindful, however, of not getting so close that you unintentionally invade the customer's space and create an uncomfortable situation for her.

Build Your Brand

Building your own personal brand has never been easier and can go a long way toward positioning you as a trusted voice in your field.

The most obvious places include various social media sites, especially LinkedIn, but there are always opportunities to volunteer in your community or join women's organizations, merchants' groups, the chamber of commerce, retail boards, and other assorted causes.

You can also write and/or share relevant content in blogs, podcasts, and other outlets to, once again, establish your voice and bona fides as a trusted and capable professional.

Love Your Customers

Be damned the stereotypes of slick-talking, sleazy salesmen in used-car lots and Hollywood movies.

One of the defining attributes of superstar salespeople is their absolute obsession with doing right by their customers. They bust through barriers and occasionally break a rule or two along the way to demonstrate their absolute commitment to serving their clients.

If you're ambivalent about people, you probably shouldn't be in sales because it is impossible to fake empathy, concern, and interest in customers, and they will see right through your schtick if you are inauthentic.

Time Versus Price

There is real value in drawing a customer's attention to the time dimension when price stressors enter the conversation. You can do that in two important, but different, ways.

In the first instance, the right choice can save the customer time, and despite spending more hours than ever on personal devices and social-media sites, people are nonetheless surprisingly stingy when it comes to their own personal time.

A second aspect of time is pointing out how the best choice will reward the customer by sustaining over time. The best products will be enjoyed long after the price is forgotten.

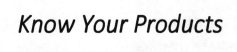

Know Your Products

While engagement rarely happens as a result of telling the customer everything you know, it is essential to have a functional knowledge of the products you are selling.

Anything less is disrespectful to your customers, your colleagues, and your managers.

A customer will generally forgive a salesperson without an encyclopedic knowledge of everything they sell, but there's no excuse for not having a basic understanding of your product offerings.

If your store does not provide formal product training, establish a routine for yourself to spend a few minutes each day familiarizing yourself with a new brand or product story. Over a period of time, you should be sufficiently conversant to engage customers on the details that matter.

Remember, however, the more you tell, the less you sell.

Small Wins Matter

Top salespeople know that closing sales is not the end result of a passive process.

It is, moreover, a series of smaller steps that carry the conversation to the final conclusion in the sales process.

Getting small affirmatives from the customer ongoing—*Yes, that color. Yes, that style is great. Yes, that is a good price range*—makes the ultimate close less intimidating.

In fact, a series of small closes can very often lead to an assumed close from both the customer and the salesperson.

Making small requests as you go, easy wins (shall I put this away so we can focus on these other two?), is also likely to mitigate defensiveness on the customer's part as they become an active and affirmative partner in the sales process.

Immediately Acknowledge Customers

Customers need to be acknowledged when they enter the store, even if all salespeople are already working with customers.

There is a certain paradox in advising you to stay in the moment when you are with a customer, while also maintaining an awareness of customers entering your store, but that is sometimes necessary.

If your colleagues are available, stay present and don't break the contact with your customer. If, however, you know that your colleagues are unavailable, you need to quietly acknowledge the customer entering your store.

This can be done with a quick smile and a nod before immediately returning your attention to the customer you are working with.

You don't need to verbally engage the person entering the store, as it could invite an exchange that will go longer than planned and irritate the client you are already working with.

Emotions Are Contagious

Knowing that emotions are contagious is a stark reminder that the mood a salesperson brings into their customer interaction will significantly influence how that customer will feel about the salesperson.

Emotions transfer more quickly than words, so no matter what a salesperson says in greeting or while working with the customer, the mood—positive, negative, or indifferent—is what the customer will respond to. This may not happen at a conscious level, but it will have an impact.

The old adage "Leave your problems at home" has real merit.

Customers should not have to guess why a given salesperson is emitting negative energy, but they will respond in kind if they pick up on it.

Conversely, if your mood is positive and upbeat, they will respond to that in a positive way.

Suggesting Add-Ons

One of the easiest ways to increase your sales is to suggest an add-on.

Some might see that as greedy or even predatory, but that couldn't be further from the truth.

If you have connected with a customer and they have trusted you enough to spend their money, the most obvious thing in the world is to ask them what other upcoming occasions they need to take care of.

At best, you'll add on another sale. At worst, you will have opened a dialogue and planted seeds for a future sale.

Don't Touch Your Neck

You do not have to be a body language expert to detect and be influenced by nonverbal signals.

One such indicator is when someone places their hand on, or strokes, their own neck.

Doing so suggests a level of discomfort and anxiety, and it can make for an extremely uncomfortable experience for the customer.

Without knowing why, the customer is put in an awkward situation, and her natural instinct is to remove herself at the earliest opportunity.

*If You're Good at Making
Excuses, You're Bad at
Making Sales*

Nobody likes to lose a sale, to miss their goals, or to disappoint themselves or their manager.

Those sentiments are universal.

In my experience, however, I have found that more successful salespeople look inward when things don't go as planned.

They are more inclined to self-examine and look for the lessons and teaching moments when things don't go their way to be better prepared for the next prospect.

They don't like defeats, but they don't waste time making excuses for their missed sales.

They're too busy planning for the next opportunity.

Don't Prejudge Customers

A salesperson who decides what a customer is capable of spending is shortsighted and presumptuous.

Customers often get a dopamine rush in advance of making an important purchase, and the easiest way to dampen that euphoria is to underestimate their ability to buy.

It is the salesperson's job to engage customers in a meaningful way and to inspire them to do things perhaps they themselves didn't know they were capable of doing when they came into your store.

Allow your customer to reach, and never decide what they are capable of spending.

Furniture Is Not Your Friend

Avoid putting furniture between you and your customer whenever possible.

Desks, display cases, and counters can all serve as physical and psychological barriers and make it more difficult to establish a connection with your customer.

If you work in an environment where you need to be behind a case to retrieve products, at the very least, try to meet the customer on the same side to welcome them and establish a rapport, and if the opportunity presents itself, return to the same side of the counter.

If Foot Traffic Is Down,
Conversion Should Be Up

Brick-and-mortar retail continues to experience declines in foot traffic that began in earnest more than a decade ago.

That reality places heavier demands on marketers and CRM professionals to be more creative in driving customers into stores, but it also presents an opportunity for salespeople.

Quite simply, if foot traffic is down in your store, your conversion rate should be up.

Less people means fewer distractions and more time to give your undivided attention to every prospect.

At its core, sales is a math game. You should know what your personal conversion rate is tracking, and one of the most effective goals you can give yourself is to improve your closing ratio.

If you have typically closed one out of every three prospects and you can increase that to one out of every two customers, you will have grown your business by 50 percent.

*Mirror Your Customer's
Rate of Speech*

If your speaking pattern is measured and deliberate, it can be physiologically jarring for your customer if he or she has a faster speaking style and demeanor.

Mirroring your customer's speaking style (faster, slower, less formal, more formal, etc.) synchronizes the neurons for both parties and facilitates a better rapport.

The more in sync you are in your speaking style, the more at ease your customer will be with you.

Embrace Silence

Western culture has never been overly friendly to silence.

In fact, more salespeople have talked themselves out of sales because they talk all over the customer's thoughts. They don't afford enough space for the customer to process what they are hearing and seeing, and the added noise serves only to invite the customer to disengage to save themselves from the incessant chatter.

When you have answered the customer's question or made your pitch, stop talking and let the customer think. They will ask you follow-up questions if they want more information, and they will give you numerous nonverbal signals if you watch closely enough.

All Sales Are Not Equal

You are not a great salesperson if you give the company's profits away to make a sale.

Frequently discounting is a bad habit of weak salespeople (who sometimes masquerade as high performers) who do not have the confidence or talent to sell the value proposition.

Few stores today can withstand prolonged margin erosion, so recognizing that every sales dollar is not equal is fundamental to sustaining a healthy business.

Know what you are selling and what products deliver the best returns to the bottom line for your business.

Work on the Customer's Timeframe

One of the enduring lessons from online shopping is not the massive amounts of options, it is the efficiency with which we can get our business done.

Customers today are very protective of their time, and, oftentimes unconsciously, they demand speed and efficiency when they visit retail stores.

If they spend time in your store browsing, it should be because they elected to do so, not because of your inefficiency.

Make sure you respect your customers' time by getting them in and out of your place of business on their timetable, not yours.

When Words and Body
Language Misalign, Words Lose

Whenever there is a disconnect between words and body language, body language wins every single time.

This is vitally important when you greet a customer, while trying to build rapport, or when attempting to overcome objections or handle rejection.

Be very aware of what your body language is communicating—I'm happy to see you, or not; I'm in a good mood, or not; you have my complete attention, or you don't—and ensure your nonverbals and words align.

Likewise, if there is a disconnect between what your customer is saying and what her body language is communicating, believe the body language every time.

Always Thank the Customer

Customers have endless choices about where and how to invest their time and money.

If they made the effort to visit your store, whether they bought something or not, sincerely thank them for giving you the opportunity to help them.

At a minimum, you will have left a positive impression and possibly laid the foundation for a future sale.

Embrace Agitated Customers

It is hardly breaking news to suggest that salespeople are not inherently drawn to agitated or upset customers. In fact, the default response is often to turn away and hope someone else will handle the problem.

Understandably, those experiences can be stressful in some situations, but they are also great opportunities to learn and improve as individuals and as businesses.

Adopting an empathic attitude and demeanor, using positive language such as "I understand you are frustrated, tell me how I can help..." or "Tell me what happened so we can get you some answers..." and physically leaning in to the customer to signal your concern will go a long way toward diffusing heated situations.

The first rule of thumb when dealing with an upset customer is to listen intently. They don't want to be challenged, corrected, or interrupted. A little effort from an empathic salesperson can work wonders with an unhappy customer and turn them into a raving fan of yours and the business thereafter.

Fish When the Fish Are Swimming

If you have the opportunity to do so, schedule your hours when your store is likely to be busiest.

Mediocre salespeople are happy to check the box and work the requisite number of hours regardless of the sales opportunities presented or lost in those hours.

Top sales performers, however, are very protective of their time and seek to cast their line when the fish are swimming. They are driven by the prospect of making sales rather than simply punching the clock, and they want to work when there are likely to be more customers in the store and more sales opportunities.

The more prospects you see, the more opportunities you have; the more opportunities you have, the more sales you make. It's math. Make it work for you.

If Your Manager Lacks Integrity...

There is an old maxim that people don't so much work for companies as they work for managers.

To that end, it is imperative that there is a safe and trusting relationship between salespeople and the store manager.

That doesn't, of course, preclude the manager from delivering tough love when it is warranted. It does, however, mean that he or she needs to be both professional and consistent in giving it.

If that is not the case, you ought to be able to address your concerns with your manager respectfully. If that doesn't redress the situation, bring your concerns to the owner of the business.

If the owner turns a blind eye to your concerns, it might be time to look for a new job.

Priming

Priming is the act of influencing consumer behavior with simple, often unconscious, cues.

In the same way that the smell of popcorn reminds us of attending movie theaters, or the aroma of coffee beans might evoke Starbucks, a question such as "Tell me about the person you are buying for" is a powerful primer that is loaded with neurological resonance.

The question is open-ended, and it is empathic ("Tell me..."), indicating your desire to listen to the customer. It also has a strong emotional component, conjuring thoughts of the gift recipient, or the reasons for the self-purchase, and it has a priming effect ("buying for..."), as we unconsciously signal to the customer that the interaction will result in a purchase.

Priming is subtle, unconscious, and highly effective.

Non-Business Rapport

Refrain from getting right to a business conversation when a customer first enters your store.

A warm welcome delivered in the form of a time-appropriate acknowledgment ("Good morning," for example) and a smile is usually the most effective greeting.

Then strike up a non-business conversation for a few moments to break the ice and establish a rapport before transitioning to the reason for the visit.

Pay attention to the customer's demeanor for signs that he or she might be in a hurry to get their business done and move on. In those situations, transition quickly to the business purpose with a simple "Tell me how I can help you..."

Walk the Talk

If you are genuinely committed to improving your own performance, then walk the talk.

Identify the strengths you wish to build upon and the shortcomings you wish to remedy, and then create a plan to address them.

That might be improving your product knowledge with formal or self-directed programs. It might be improving your client-outreach efforts. It could be finding a mentor to help you grow and develop.

Saying you want to improve your performance and having no plan to do so is a recipe for stagnation, not growth.

Be a Team Player, But...

Being a team player doesn't mean subverting your own ambitions and talents to fit in with a group.

It means each person doing what they do best within the context of a team environment.

It means being respectful and civil to your colleagues, but it doesn't mean diluting your strengths to satisfy lesser performers' desire to prevent anyone from exposing their shortcomings.

If you're the quarterback, play quarterback. If you are a lineman, block.

Don't compromise your drive and ambition because it upsets mediocre teammates.

The Paradox of Dominant Emotions

I've written about the power of getting in sync with your customer throughout this book. That means aligning your gestures, your tone of voice, your rate of speech, and your body language.

There is one important caveat.

When your customer is in a negative, or perhaps even agitated, state, you must maintain a positive attitude and demeanor. Keep a smile on your face, listen intently, and continue to use positive language.

Your optimistic state will begin to influence your customer's demeanor toward positivity. Scientists call this "emotional contagion," and it is a transference of (dominant) emotions from one person to another.

If You Want a Better
Vocabulary...

Some people seem to be blessed with the ability to say just the right thing at the right moment.

They seem to have a remarkable capacity with words and an almost unfair advantage over people who are less erudite.

No matter what your level of education, the single best way to improve your vocabulary is to read. And the best way to make major improvements is to read a lot.

Don't get hung up believing you need to read business books, sales books, or celebrated literary masterpieces. Read what is exciting to you.

Experiment with different books and authors, and find what you love to read.

He Who Listens the Most

It's ironic that after meeting someone new, people often come away raving about how interesting the stranger was without recalling anything of note that they actually said.

Upon reflection, they often realize that the person they met was interesting not because of what was said but because he or she was a great listener.

People want to be listened to. And the more you listen by giving that person your complete attention, by nodding, leaning in, and occasional providing subtle verbal affirmation, the more they feel respected.

By relinquishing the control that comes from speaking or, worse, pontificating, we actually gain power—the power of presence and respect.

Nobody has ever had to apologize for listening too much.

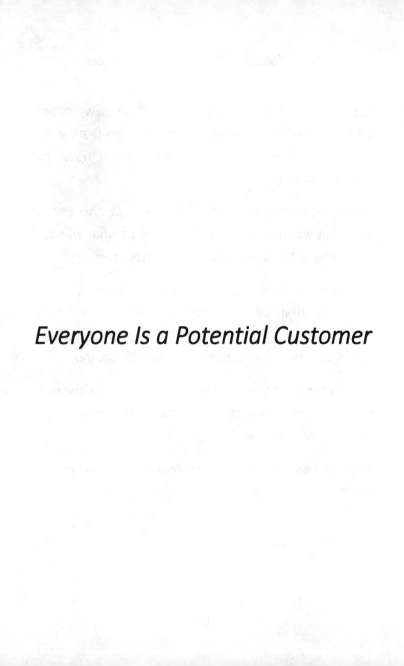

Everyone Is a Potential Customer

Everyone who enters your store is a potential customer and should be treated accordingly.

That includes the UPS and FedEx delivery people and any service folks who stop in to conduct business.

Investing the time to acknowledge and engage all visitors to your store costs little, shows great respect for the people who are visiting, and will occasionally lead to sales.

Don't exclude anyone as a potential customer.

Showing Gratitude

Showing appreciation to your customers should be self-evident and practiced habitually.

Beyond thanking customers for their business, you should also thank customers who took the trouble to bring concerns to your attention.

And finally, find ways to show your appreciation to your colleagues whenever it is warranted.

Civility is contagious and best served in small and frequent doses.

*Your Body Language Will Lead
Your Mind-Set*

We have long known that our body language reflects how we feel. If I am happy, that will show in my body language. If I am sad, depressed, or agitated, that too will be reflected in my body language.

Less obvious are the effects that positive and open body language can have on your attitude and demeanor. In fact, your body language can actually lead your mind-set and attitude.

If you are feeling low energy, move around instead of sitting or slouching.

Think about your posture; straighten your spine, open your hands, keep your head up, and wear a smile on your face.

You'll find that specific, conscious, physical actions will help change your mood and pull you into a more positive place.

Discounts Requests

If your business practices a fixed-price strategy and you are asked for a discount, reply that you *don't* discount, not you *can't* discount.

There is an enormous difference between *don't* and *can't*. The latter implies that you agree that the price is not reasonable, and you wish you could offer a discount. The former asserts that your prices are appropriate and fair.

Maintain open body language and a positive demeanor, and respectfully move the conversation back to the value proposition.

Don't Say No

There is rarely ever a need to say no to a customer.

Virtually any question, from a discount request to an expedited delivery or service demand, to a request for a brand you don't carry can be answered without saying no.

If the request cannot be accommodated, you can usually reply with "Let me tell you what we can do..." or "Here's why that might not be the best idea..." or "A wonderful brand we do carry is..."

Strike no from your customer vocabulary, and replace it with more positive language.

Buying Signals

If you are completely present, if you are keenly observing your customer's body language, if you are intently listening to their words, you will pick up on important buying signals.

These gestures, which can include subtle nodding, a relaxed posture, an easy smile, or laser focus on a particular product, may even be happening at a subconscious level for the customer.

Or the clues might be more overt, such as an inquiry about delivery times, warranties, or care and handling instructions for the product.

When you sense buying signals, lead the conversation to its satisfactory conclusion by using assumptive language and close the sale.

*Don't Bad-Mouth Your
Competitors*

There is nothing more off-putting than listening to a salesperson bad-mouth their competitors.

Noting a legitimate point of differentiation is okay, but bad-mouthing another business is a bad business strategy and reflects poorly on the offending salesperson and their store.

If a customer brings up your competition, say that you are sure they are very nice people and reiterate that you will be pleased to cater to the customer's needs if they choose to trust you with their business.

Share Success Stories

Sales teams should make a habit of sharing success stories with each other.

I'm not talking about the run-of-the-mill stuff that pollutes many meetings, but specific "Here's what happened, and this is what I did that led to a sale" retellings that are both instructive and inspiring.

When you break down sales into their component parts, there is usually a great deal of learning to be gleaned: how the salesperson uncovered the customer's motivation, how they respectfully established the budget, how they overcame objections, and, ultimately, how they effected the close.

Dissecting the elements of successful sales transactions can be mini master classes.

Wear Your Club Colors

You are an ambassador for your business, and you ought to act that way.

Do not talk about your company in the third person. If you find yourself using the word, *'they'* when describing policies, procedures, or aspects of the business you might not agree with, you need to re-calibrate or relocate.

Cultural negativity is a cancer that spreads and reinforces the worst instincts in people.

Every company has issues from time to time. When they happen, address them respectfully with the appropriate people in the right way. Don't exacerbate them by blowing them out of proportion and feeding the noise.

Be the solution, not the problem.

Prioritize Selling Time

Prioritizing selling time should be as fundamental as brushing your teeth in the morning, and yet far too many salespeople are content to do anything but sell throughout the course of their day.

They create busywork ("Hey, someone's got to tidy up the cases!") with the assumption that it has the same value to the business as sales activity.

Making sales should be priority number 1, 2, and 3.

Everything else comes next.

So, if you find yourself more often drawn to the behind-the-scenes work, redoing displays, stocking shelves, repricing products, etc., ask yourself if you are cut out for a career in sales.

Pucker Those Lips

Biting your lower lip, or retracting your lips entirely, can be perceived as a stress behavior.

If you are doing either while presenting a product solution, or after you have given a price, the customer may perceive that you lack confidence in what you are offering.

Try to maintain a Mona Lisa smile (subtle, barely detectable) while you are presenting a product or price.

Your smile may be slight, but it will prevent you from hiding your lips and unintentionally communicating, or even transferring, your anxiety to your customers.

Touching the Product

Encouraging your customers to try on or touch your products substantially increases their propensity to purchase the goods.

In handling the products, customers can experience a boost of serotonin (the reward and happiness hormone) in anticipation of owning the items.

It can also elevate the perceived value of the product in the eyes of the customer.

So, get that item into the customer's hands, or on their body, and marvel as they fall in love with it and help you to close a sale.

Popular and Scarce

Telling customers that a product is popular delivers a psychological safety net that removes some of the anxiety of shopping. Telling them that it is popular *and* scarce is even more compelling.

Clients, at their core, are anxious to avoid making the wrong decision (regret avoidance). Letting them know that people love a given product eases that burden. It is what social psychologists call "social proof," the idea that if other people are buying the product, it must be okay.

If you also tell the customer that the product is scarce, it ignites their fear of losing out—an emotion that overwhelms less persuasive buying triggers.

Word to the wise: be honest. If you are saying a product is popular and scare when that is not true, you've got an integrity problem.

Prospecting Is Never
One and Done

Prospecting is not a one-and-done exercise.

It has been said that we need to touch a prospect seven times on average to produce a positive result. One can debate the merits of that in all situations, but what is certain is that salespeople must be prepared to make frequent outreach efforts to prospective customers.

That could be through invitations to store events, a note about an arriving new brand or collection, a heads-up about an upcoming sale, or a reminder to have a product checked or cleaned.

The outreach should be spread over an appropriate period of time to make it easier for customers to think of you when an occasion to buy presents itself, while not alienating her with countless self-serving outreaches that become spam to the customer.

*Each Rejection Is a Step
Closer to a Sale*

Nobody, not even superstar salespeople, will be successful with 100 percent of their customers 100 percent of the time.

In reality, they probably experience more rejection than their colleagues because they put themselves in front of more prospects, and they ask for the sale more often.

To be successful in sales, you need to be okay with rejection—lots of rejection. But each rejection you receive gets you one step closer to the next sale.

And that, when all is said and done, is what this whole ball of wax is about.

CPSIA information can be obtained
at www.ICGtesting.com
Printed in the USA
BVHW030858120721
R12399400002B/R123994PG611565BVX00020B/7

And in the End...

Professional sales development does not require wholesale changes in your approach, and it doesn't mean discarding the good habits and traits that have made you successful to date.

It does, however, require frequent and deliberate small improvements to expand your sales effectiveness and deliver better results. Helping you to make those small improvements was the reason I wrote this book, and why I chose the shorter format.

If you've made it this far, thank you for reading *The Sales Minute*. I hope you found some of the tips and pointers helpful. I also hope you will use it as a companion piece and return to it from time to time.

If you enjoyed the book, I'd appreciate a quick review on Amazon, Goodreads, or your preferred book platform.

I'd also love to hear what you thought of the book.

You can connect with me on LinkedIn, on my website, theretailsmiths.com, or at Dublinsmith@yahoo.com.

With appreciation,

Peter Smith